SUPER SANDCASTLE
Super Simple Cooking

Super Simple
Lunches

Easy No-Bake Recipes for Kids

Nancy Tuminelly

Consulting Editor, Diane Craig, M.A./Reading Specialist

ABDO
Publishing Company

Published by ABDO Publishing Company, 8000 West 78th Street, Edina, Minnesota 55439. Copyright © 2011 by Abdo Consulting Group, Inc. International copyrights reserved in all countries. No part of this book may be reproduced in any form without written permission from the publisher. Super SandCastle™ is a trademark and logo of ABDO Publishing Company.

Printed in the United States of America, North Mankato, Minnesota
052010
092010

 PRINTED ON RECYCLED PAPER

Editor: Katherine Hengel
Content Developer: Nancy Tuminelly
Cover and Interior Design and Production: Colleen Dolphin, Mighty Media
Photo Credits: Colleen Dolphin, iStockphoto (Pathathai Chungyam, Tammy Bryngelson, Dawna Stafford), Shutterstock
Food Production: Colleen Dolphin, Kelly Dolphin

The following manufacturers/names appearing in this book are trademarks:
Target® Plastic Wrap, Pyrex® Measuring Cup, Cholula® Hot Sauce

Library of Congress Cataloging-in-Publication Data

Tuminelly, Nancy, 1952-
   Super simple lunches : easy no-bake recipes for kids / Nancy Tuminelly.
      p. cm. -- (Super simple cooking)
   ISBN 978-1-61613-387-0
   1. Luncheons--Juvenile literature. 2. Quick and easy cookery--Juvenile literature. I. Title.
   TX735.T95 2011
   641.5'3--dc22
                          2009053192

Super SandCastle™ books are created by a team of professional educators, reading specialists, and content developers around five essential components—phonemic awareness, phonics, vocabulary, text comprehension, and fluency—to assist young readers as they develop reading skills and strategies and increase their general knowledge. All books are written, reviewed, and leveled for guided reading, early reading intervention, and Accelerated Reader® programs for use in shared, guided, and independent reading and writing activities to support a balanced approach to literacy instruction.

Note to Adult Helpers

Helping kids learn how to cook is fun! It is a great way for them to practice math and science. Cooking teaches kids about responsibility and boosts their confidence. Plus, they learn how to help out in the kitchen! The recipes in this book require very little adult assistance. But make sure there is always an adult around when kids are in the kitchen. Expect kids to make a mess, but also expect them to clean up after themselves. Most importantly, make the experience pleasurable by sharing and enjoying the food kids make.

Symbols

 knife
Always ask an adult to help you cut with knives.

 keep it cold!
If you take this dish to go, use a cooler to keep it cold.

 nuts
Some people can get very sick if they eat nuts.

Contents

Let's Cook!

The recipes in this book are simple! You don't even need an oven or stove! Cooking teaches you about food, measuring, and following directions. It's fun to make good food! Enjoy your tasty creations with family and friends!

Bon appétit!

Cooking Basics

Before You Start...

- Get permission from an adult.
- Wash your hands.
- Read the recipe at least once.
- Set out all the ingredients, tools, and equipment you will need.
- Keep a towel close by for cleaning up spills.

When You're Done...

- Cover food with plastic wrap or **aluminum** foil. Use containers with tops when you can.
- Put all the ingredients and tools back where you found them.
- Wash all the dishes and **utensils**.
- Clean up your work space.

THINK SAFETY!

- Ask an adult to help you cut things. Use a cutting board.
- Clean up spills to prevent accidents.
- Keep tools and **utensils** away from the edge of the table or countertop.
- Use a **sturdy** stool if you cannot reach something.

Packing a Lunch is Fun!

- Use zip top plastic bags and **airtight** containers.
- Use freezer gel packs or plastic ice cubes. Some foods spoil if they get too warm.
- Wipe out your lunch bag after school every day.
- Decorate your lunch bag. Show your style!

Reduce, Reuse, Recycle!

When it comes to helping the earth, little things add up! Here are some ways to go green in the kitchen!

- Reuse plastic bags. If they aren't too dirty, you can use them again!
- Take a lunchbox. Then you won't use a paper bag.
- Store food in reusable containers instead of using plastic bags.
- Carry a reusable water bottle. Then you won't buy drinks all the time!

Measuring Tips

Wet Ingredients
Set a measuring cup on the countertop. Add the liquid until it reaches the amount you need. Check the measurement from eye level.

Dry Ingredients
Dip the measuring cup or spoon into the dry ingredient. Scoop out a little more than you need. Use the back of a dinner knife to scrape off the **excess**.

Moist Ingredients
Ingredients like brown sugar and dried fruit are a little different. They need to be packed down into the measuring cup. Keep packing until the ingredient reaches your measurement line.

Do You Know This = That?

There are different ways to measure the same amount.

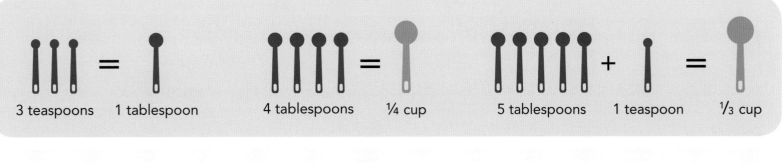

3 teaspoons = 1 tablespoon

4 tablespoons = ¼ cup

5 tablespoons + 1 teaspoon = ⅓ cup

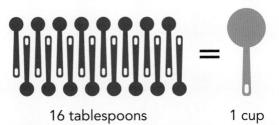

16 tablespoons = 1 cup

1 cup = 8 ounces

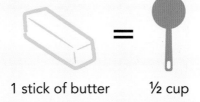

1 stick of butter = ½ cup

2 cups = 1 pint

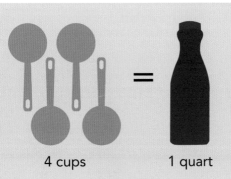

4 cups = 1 quart

2 quarts = ½ gallon

Cooking Terms

Chop
Cut into very small pieces with a knife.

Dice
Cut into small cubes with a knife.

Grate
Shred food into small pieces with a grater.

Mix
Combine ingredients with a mixing spoon.

Slice

Cut into thin pieces with a knife.

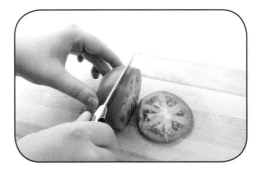

Mash

Crush food until soft with fork or masher.

Folding a Tortilla

1. Place tortilla on flat surface. Add filling. Make it about as wide as three fingers. Keep it at least three fingers away from edge.

2. Fold one edge over filling.

3. Fold one long side over the top of filling. Put fingers across fold and push edge against filling. Wrap other long end over both folds.

4. Turn burrito over with folded side down. Let rest for a minute to make sure it stays closed.

Tools

 Here are some of the tools that you'll need to get started.

mixing spoon

strainer

grater

mixing bowls

spoon

measuring cups
(dry ingredients)

measuring cup
(wet ingredients)

measuring spoons

can opener

plate

plastic wrap

whisk

cutting board

vegetable peeler

fork

dinner knife

sharp knife

toothpicks

Ingredients

Fresh Produce

- [ ] romaine lettuce
- [ ] carrots
- [ ] green peppers
- [ ] mushrooms
- [ ] tomatoes
- [ ] red grapes
- [ ] iceberg lettuce
- [ ] celery
- [ ] red bell peppers
- [ ] garlic cloves
- [ ] parsley sprigs
- [ ] cucumbers
- [ ] onions
- [ ] green onions

- [ ] fresh cilantro
- [ ] apples
- [ ] fresh spinach

Canned Goods

- [ ] pineapple chunks
- [ ] water chestnuts
- [ ] kidney beans
- [ ] chickpeas
- [ ] tuna
- [ ] cranberry sauce

Dairy

- [ ] swiss cheese, grated
- [ ] mozzarella cheese
- [ ] provolone cheese

Meat

- [ ] deli turkey
- [ ] chicken
- [ ] ham

Other

- [ ] whole-wheat tortillas
- [ ] mayonnaise
- [ ] ranch salad dressing
- [ ] whole-wheat pitas
- [ ] pocket-style pita rounds
- [ ] salad dressing (any kind)
- [ ] vegetable oil

- [ ] white vinegar
- [ ] lemon juice
- [ ] crackers
- [ ] toasted sesame oil
- [ ] hot pepper sauce
- [ ] flour tortillas
- [ ] honey
- [ ] salt
- [ ] pepper
- [ ] pecans

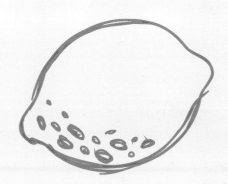

13

Gobble-Gobble Wrap

Now that's a wrap!

Makes 1 serving

Ingredients

1 medium whole-wheat tortilla

1 tablespoon mayonnaise

1½ tablespoons cranberry sauce

3 slices deli turkey

2 romaine lettuce leaves

2 teaspoons pecans, chopped

Tools

• plate

• measuring spoons

• dinner knife

• spoon

• can opener

• sharp knife

• cutting board

1. Lay tortilla flat on plate. Spread mayonnaise on tortilla. Then spoon cranberry sauce down center.

2. Put folded turkey slices, lettuce leaves, and chopped pecans on top of cranberry sauce.

3. Fold as shown.

Very Veggie Pockets

A delicious way to eat vegetables!

Makes 2 servings

Ingredients

⅓ cup carrots, grated

⅓ cup green pepper, chopped

⅓ cup mushrooms, sliced

2 tablespoons salad dressing (any kind)

2 pocket-style pita rounds

⅓ cup tomatoes, sliced

1 cup Swiss cheese, grated

Tools

- sharp knife
- cutting board
- measuring cups
- measuring spoons
- medium bowl
- mixing spoon
- grater
- plates

1. Mix carrots, green pepper, mushrooms, and salad dressing in medium bowl.

2. Cut each pita in half and open to make pockets. Put an even amount of vegetables in each pocket half. Add tomato slices.

3. Sprinkle ¼ cup Swiss cheese into each pocket half.

4. Put pocket halves on plate.

Chicken Salad Pitas

The sweetest chicken salad ever!

Makes 6 servings

Ingredients

2 cups cooked chicken, diced

½ cup celery, chopped

½ cup water chestnuts, drained and chopped

2 tablespoons red bell pepper, chopped

8-ounce can pineapple chunks, drained

1 cup red grapes, sliced

⅔ cup ranch salad dressing

6 pocket-style pita rounds

12 iceberg lettuce leaves

Tools

- strainer
- measuring cups and spoons
- can opener
- sharp knife
- cutting board
- large bowl
- mixing spoon
- plastic wrap

1 Mix all ingredients except pita bread and lettuce in large bowl with mixing spoon.

2 Cover bowl with **airtight** lid or plastic wrap. Put salad mixture in refrigerator for at least 4 hours.

3 Cut each pita in half. Stuff one lettuce leaf into each pita half. Spoon some salad mixture into each pita half.

You can use **leftover** chicken in this recipe! Deli chicken or **rotisserie** chicken works too.

Lean Bean Salad

A unique salad to eat at lunchtime!

Makes 2 servings

Ingredients

8-ounce can kidney beans, drained

1 tomato, chopped

1 small onion, chopped

1 tablespoon vegetable oil

1 teaspoon white vinegar

1 clove garlic, mashed

salt and pepper

1 sprig of parsley, chopped

Tools

• strainer
• can opener
• sharp knife
• cutting board
• mixing bowls
• mixing spoon
• measuring spoons
• whisk
• 2 serving bowls

1. **Drain** kidney beans and rinse under cold water.

2. Mix kidney beans, tomatoes, and onions in medium bowl with mixing spoon.

3. Stir oil, vinegar, garlic, and a little salt and pepper together in small bowl with whisk.

4. Pour oil mixture over vegetables and mix together well.

5. Put an equal amount of bean mixture in each bowl. Sprinkle parsley on top.

21

Tossed Salad Pitas

Veggies make this a pleasure to eat!

Makes 2 servings

Ingredients

2 pocket-style pita rounds

1 cup lettuce or spinach, rinsed and shredded

¼ cup red bell pepper, chopped

¼ cup cucumber, chopped

¼ cup carrots, peeled and shredded

¼ cup canned chickpeas, drained and rinsed

¼ cup mozzarella cheese, shredded

½ cup salad dressing (any kind)

Tools

- sharp knife
- cutting board
- two plates
- measuring cups
- strainer
- can opener
- large bowl
- mixing spoon
- forks

1. Cut each pita in half and put two halves on each plate.

2. Mix all remaining ingredients except cheese and salad dressing in large bowl.

3. Use two forks to stir cheese and dressing into salad mixture.

4. Fill each pita half with some salad mixture and serve.

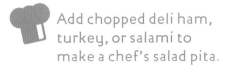 Add chopped deli ham, turkey, or salami to make a chef's salad pita.

Tasty Tuna Salad

An old favorite that's always great!

Makes 2 servings

Ingredients

5-ounce can tuna, drained

1 tablespoon onion, chopped

1 tablespoon celery, chopped

¼ teaspoon lemon juice

1 tablespoon mayonnaise

salt and pepper

crackers

two iceberg lettuce leaves

1 tomato, sliced

Tools

- can opener
- fork
- medium bowl
- measuring spoons
- sharp knife
- cutting board
- mixing spoon
- small bowl
- spoon
- plates

1. Put tuna in medium bowl and mash with fork.

2. Stir onions and celery into tuna. Mix well with spoon.

3. Stir lemon juice and mayonnaise together in small bowl. Pour onto tuna mixture and stir well with spoon. Add a little salt and pepper.

4. Spoon tuna mixture on top of some iceberg lettuce leaves. Serve with crackers and tomato slices.

For extra flavor, add 1 tablespoon pickle relish, chopped hard-boiled eggs, or chopped cucumbers!

25

Aso Tuna Burritos

Tuna salad with an Asian flavor!

Makes 2 servings

Ingredients

5-ounce can tuna, drained

2 tablespoons mayonnaise

1 tablespoon green onion, chopped

1 tablespoon celery, chopped

1 tablespoon carrot, shredded

1 tablespoon fresh cilantro, chopped

½ teaspoon toasted sesame oil

salt and pepper

2 whole-wheat tortillas

hot pepper sauce (optional)

Tools

• can opener

• strainer

• measuring spoons

• sharp knife and cutting board

• medium bowl

• mixing spoon

• plates

1. Mix tuna, mayonnaise, green onion, celery, carrot, cilantro, oil, and a little salt and pepper in a medium bowl.

2. Stir a few drops of hot pepper sauce into tuna mixture if desired.

3. Lay each tortilla flat on plate. Spoon ½ tuna mixture onto center of each tortilla. Fold to make burrito.

To learn how to fold a tortilla, see page 9.

Ham & Cheese Pinwheels

Try a spin on this lunch special!

Makes 4 servings

Ingredients

¼ cup mayonnaise
or salad dressing

2 cloves garlic, minced

2 large flour tortillas

1 cup fresh spinach, rinsed

4 slices ham

6 slices provolone cheese

1 medium tomato, sliced

Tools

• measuring cups

• small bowl

• spoon

• plate

• measuring spoon

• strainer

• sharp knife

• cutting board

• toothpicks

1. Mix mayonnaise and **minced** garlic together in small bowl.

2. Lay each tortilla on a plate. Spread 1 tablespoon mayonnaise mixture over each tortilla.

3. Top tortillas with spinach, ham, cheese, and tomato slices.

4. Roll each tortilla tightly. Cut in half. Push toothpick through each half to hold it together.

29

Carrot-Apple Rollups

A quick and nutritious lunchtime treat!

Makes 2 servings

Ingredients

¼ cup carrot, peeled and grated

¼ cup cheddar cheese, grated

1 apple

1 tablespoon honey

2 whole-wheat or flour tortillas

Tools

- vegetable peeler
- sharp knife
- cutting board
- grater
- measuring cups
- measuring spoons
- medium bowl
- mixing spoon
- plate
- plastic wrap

1. **Peel** and core apple. Cut apple in half. Grate one of the halves.

2. Mix grated carrot, cheese, and apple together in medium bowl. Stir in honey and mix well.

3. Lay each tortilla flat on a plate. Spoon mixture on one end of each tortilla.

4. Roll up tortillas. Wrap rolls tightly in plastic wrap. Put in refrigerator for at least 20 minutes before eating.

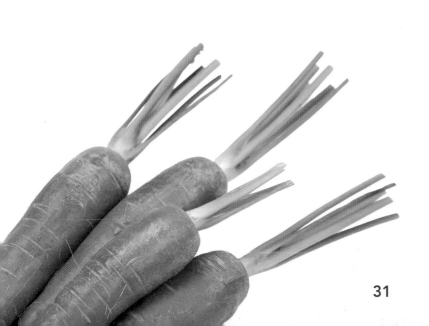

Glossary

airtight – so well sealed that no air can get in or out.

aluminum – a light metal.

drain – to remove liquid using a strainer.

excess – more than the amount wanted or needed.

leftover – something remaining.

minced – chopped into very small pieces.

peel – to remove the skin or outer covering of a vegetable or fruit.

rotisserie – cooked on a spit that rotates over heat.

sturdy – strong and well built.

utensil – a tool used to prepare or eat food.